T5-BSJ-777

Unfolding the Truth

– ONE BOOK AT A TIME –

Galatians

Lisa Meiners

Copyright © 2012 by Lisa Meiners.
All rights reserved. This book or any portion thereof
may not be reproduced or used in any manner whatsoever
without the express written permission of the publisher
except for the use of brief quotations in a book review.

Printed in the United States of America

Second Printing, 2012

ISBN 978-1-4675-4952-3

Design and printing by Fairhaven Church
637 E. Whipp Road, Centerville, OH 45459
www.fairhavenchurch.org

Unless otherwise noted, Scripture quotations are taken from the
New American Standard Bible® (NASB). Copyright © 1960, 1962, 1963,
1968, 1971, 1972, 1973, 1975, 1977, 1995 by The Lockman Foundation.
Used with permission. (www.Lockman.org)

TABLE OF CONTENTS

WELCOME TO GALATIANS!

Many of us have taken a memorable trip that has impacted us in some fashion. My hope is for you to be impacted, in a lasting way, as we travel through "Unfolding the Truth: Galatians."

Galatians may be a short letter from Paul to the believers in Galatia, but inside the six chapters Paul demonstrates his passion for both the Gospel and the Galatians as he instructs them and us.

Traveling through Galatians chapter-by-chapter, verse-by-verse, and word-by-word has filled me to overflowing. Along the way I discovered many mile markers I cannot wait to share with you.

My goal is to make studying God's Word interactive and memorable for those who travel with me.

- Through various **learning activities** I anticipate unfolding fundamental truths to equip you for your faith journey.

- Marking **key words** each week and studying **various translations** of the text will provide a broader understanding as you travel verse-by-verse.

- Wrapped inside each lesson will be challenging and thought provoking **application questions**. As you reflect on these you will be drawn DEEPER STILL in your personal study time.

- Finally, at the conclusion of each lesson you will be asked to choose a **memory verse** to learn. At the end you will have six verses hidden in your heart to strengthen you for your journey.

My prayer for your next six weeks comes from Colossians 2:6: Abba, let your daughter's roots grow down into You, drawing up nourishment so she will grow in faith, strong and vigorous in the truth she will be taught. Amen.

Sincerely looking forward to studying God's Word with you,

1 Paul, an apostle (not sent from men nor through the agency of man, but through Jesus Christ and God the Father, who raised Him from the dead), 2 and all the brethren who are with me, To the churches of Galatia:

3 Grace to you and peace from God our Father and the Lord Jesus Christ, 4 who gave Himself for our sins so that He might rescue us from this present evil age, according to the will of our God and Father, 5 to whom be the glory forevermore. Amen.

6 I am amazed that you are so quickly deserting Him who called you by the grace of Christ, for a different gospel; 7 which is really not another; only there are some who are disturbing you and want to distort the gospel of Christ. 8 But even if we, or an angel from heaven, should preach to you a gospel contrary to what we have preached to you, he is to be accursed! 9 As we have said before, so I say again now, if any man is preaching to you a gospel contrary to what you received, he is to be accursed!

10 For am I now seeking the favor of men, or of God? Or am I striving to please men? If I were still trying to please men, I would not be a bond-servant of Christ.

11 For I would have you know, brethren, that the gospel which was preached by me is not according to man. 12 For I neither received it from man, nor was I taught it, but I received it through a revelation of Jesus Christ.

13 For you have heard of my former manner of life in Judaism, how I used to persecute the church of God beyond measure and tried to destroy it; 14 and I was advancing in Judaism beyond many of my contemporaries among my countrymen, being more extremely zealous for my ancestral traditions. 15 But when God, who had set me apart

even from my mother's womb and called me through His grace, was pleased 16 to reveal His Son in me so that I might preach Him among the Gentiles, I did not immediately consult with flesh and blood, 17 nor did I go up to Jerusalem to those who were apostles before me; but I went away to Arabia, and returned once more to Damascus.

18 Then three years later I went up to Jerusalem to become acquainted with Cephas, and stayed with him fifteen days. 19 But I did not see any other of the apostles except James, the Lord's brother. 20 (Now in what I am writing to you, I assure you before God that I am not lying.) 21 Then I went into the regions of Syria and Cilicia. 22 I was still unknown by sight to the churches of Judea which were in Christ; 23 but only, they kept hearing, "He who once persecuted us is now preaching the faith which he once tried to destroy." 24 And they were glorifying God because of me.

1 Then after an interval of fourteen years I went up again to Jerusalem with Barnabas, taking Titus along also. 2 It was because of a revelation that I went up; and I submitted to them the gospel which I preach among the Gentiles, but I did so in private to those who were of reputation, for fear that I might be running, or had run, in vain. 3 But not even Titus, who was with me, though he was a Greek, was compelled to be circumcised. 4 But it was because of the false brethren secretly brought in, who had sneaked in to spy out our liberty which we have in Christ Jesus, in order to bring us into bondage. 5 But we did not yield in subjection to them for even an hour, so that the truth of the gospel would remain with you. 6 But from those who were of high reputation (what they were makes no difference to me; God shows no partiality)—well, those who were of reputation contributed nothing to me. 7 But on the contrary, seeing that I had been entrusted with the gospel to the uncircumcised, just as Peter had been to the circumcised 8 (for He who effectually worked for Peter in his apostleship to the circumcised effectually worked for me also to the Gentiles), 9 and recognizing the grace that had been given to me, James and Cephas and John, who were reputed to be pillars, gave to me and Barnabas the right hand of fellowship, so that we might go to the Gentiles and they to the circumcised. 10 They only asked us to remember the poor—the very thing I also was eager to do.

11 But when Cephas came to Antioch, I opposed him to his face, because he stood condemned. 12 For prior to the coming of certain men from James, he used to eat with the Gentiles; but when they came, he began to withdraw and hold himself aloof, fearing the party of the circumcision. 13 The rest of the Jews joined him in hypocrisy, with the result that even Barnabas was carried away by their hypocrisy. 14 But when I saw that they were

not straightforward about the truth of the gospel, I said to Cephas in the presence of all, "If you, being a Jew, live like the Gentiles and not like the Jews, how is it that you compel the Gentiles to live like Jews?

15 "We are Jews by nature and not sinners from among the Gentiles; 16 nevertheless knowing that a man is not justified by the works of the Law but through faith in Christ Jesus, even we have believed in Christ Jesus, so that we may be justified by faith in Christ and not by the works of the Law; since by the works of the Law no flesh will be justified. 17 "But if, while seeking to be justified in Christ, we ourselves have also been found sinners, is Christ then a minister of sin? May it never be! 18 "For if I rebuild what I have once destroyed, I prove myself to be a transgressor. 19 "For through the Law I died to the Law, so that I might live to God. 20 "I have been crucified with Christ; and it is no longer I who live, but Christ lives in me; and the life which I now live in the flesh I live by faith in the Son of God, who loved me and gave Himself up for me. 21 "I do not nullify the grace of God, for if righteousness comes through the Law, then Christ died needlessly."

1 You foolish Galatians, who has bewitched you, before whose eyes Jesus Christ was publicly portrayed as crucified? 2 This is the only thing I want to find out from you: did you receive the Spirit by the works of the Law, or by hearing with faith? 3 Are you so foolish? Having begun by the Spirit, are you now being perfected by the flesh? 4 Did you suffer so many things in vain—if indeed it was in vain? 5 So then, does He who provides you with the Spirit and works miracles among you, do it by the works of the Law, or by hearing with faith?

6 Even so Abraham BELIEVED GOD, AND IT WAS RECKONED TO HIM AS RIGHTEOUSNESS. 7 Therefore, be sure that it is those who are of faith who are sons of Abraham. 8 The Scripture, foreseeing that God would justify the Gentiles by faith, preached the gospel beforehand to Abraham, saying, "ALL THE NATIONS WILL BE BLESSED IN YOU." 9 So then those who are of faith are blessed with Abraham, the believer.

10 For as many as are of the works of the Law are under a curse; for it is written, "CURSED IS EVERYONE WHO DOES NOT ABIDE BY ALL THINGS WRITTEN IN THE BOOK OF THE LAW, TO PERFORM THEM." 11 Now that no one is justified by the Law before God is evident; for, "THE RIGHTEOUS MAN SHALL LIVE BY FAITH." 12 However, the Law is not of faith; on the contrary, "HE WHO PRACTICES THEM SHALL LIVE BY THEM." 13 Christ redeemed us from the curse of the Law, having become a curse for us—for it is written, "CURSED IS EVERYONE WHO HANGS ON A TREE"— 14 in order that in Christ Jesus the blessing of Abraham might come to the Gentiles, so that we would receive the promise of the Spirit through faith.

15 Brethren, I speak in terms of human relations: even though it is only a man's covenant, yet when it has been ratified, no one sets it aside or adds conditions to it. 16 Now the promises were spoken to Abraham and to his seed. He does not say, "And to seeds," as referring to many, but rather to one, "And to your seed," that is, Christ. 17 What I am saying is this: the Law, which came four hundred and thirty years later, does not invalidate a covenant previously ratified by God, so as to nullify the promise. 18 For if the inheritance is based on law, it is no longer based on a promise; but God has granted it to Abraham by means of a promise.

19 Why the Law then? It was added because of transgressions, having been ordained through angels by the agency of a mediator, until the seed would come to whom the promise had been made. 20 Now a mediator is not for one party only; whereas God is only one. 21 Is the Law then contrary to the promises of God? May it never be! For if a law had been given which was able to impart life, then righteousness would indeed have been based on law. 22 But the Scripture has shut up everyone under sin, so that the promise by faith in Jesus Christ might be given to those who believe.

23 But before faith came, we were kept in custody under the law, being shut up to the faith which was later to be revealed. 24 Therefore the Law has become our tutor to lead us to Christ, so that we may be justified by faith. 25 But now that faith has come, we are no longer under a tutor. 26 For you are all sons of God through faith in Christ Jesus. 27 For all of you who were baptized into Christ have clothed yourselves with Christ. 28 There is neither Jew nor Greek, there is neither slave nor free man, there is neither male nor female; for you are all one in Christ Jesus. 29 And if you belong to Christ, then you are Abraham's descendants, heirs according to promise.

GALATIANS 4

1 Now I say, as long as the heir is a child, he does not differ at all from a slave although he is owner of everything, 2 but he is under guardians and managers until the date set by the father. 3 So also we, while we were children, were held in bondage under the elemental things of the world. 4 But when the fullness of the time came, God sent forth His Son, born of a woman, born under the Law, 5 so that He might redeem those who were under the Law, that we might receive the adoption as sons. 6 Because you are sons, God has sent forth the Spirit of His Son into our hearts, crying, "Abba! Father!" 7 Therefore you are no longer a slave, but a son; and if a son, then an heir through God.

8 However at that time, when you did not know God, you were slaves to those which by nature are no gods. 9 But now that you have come to know God, or rather to be known by God, how is it that you turn back again to the weak and worthless elemental things, to which you desire to be enslaved all over again? 10 You observe days and months and seasons and years. 11 I fear for you, that perhaps I have labored over you in vain.

12 I beg of you, brethren, become as I am, for I also have become as you are. You have done me no wrong; 13 but you know that it was because of a bodily illness that I preached the gospel to you the first time; 14 and that which was a trial to you in my bodily condition you did not despise or loathe, but you received me as an angel of God, as Christ Jesus Himself. 15 Where then is that sense of blessing you had? For I bear you witness that, if possible, you would have plucked out your eyes and given them to me. 16 So have I become your enemy by telling you the truth? 17 They eagerly seek you, not commendably, but they wish to shut you out so that you will seek them. 18 But it is good always to be eagerly sought in a commendable manner, and not only when I am

present with you. **19** My children, with whom I am again in labor until Christ is formed in you— **20** but I could wish to be present with you now and to change my tone, for I am perplexed about you.

21 Tell me, you who want to be under law, do you not listen to the law? **22** For it is written that Abraham had two sons, one by the bondwoman and one by the free woman. **23** But the son by the bondwoman was born according to the flesh, and the son by the free woman through the promise. **24** This is allegorically speaking, for these women are two covenants: one proceeding from Mount Sinai bearing children who are to be slaves; she is Hagar. **25** Now this Hagar is Mount Sinai in Arabia and corresponds to the present Jerusalem, for she is in slavery with her children. **26** But the Jerusalem above is free; she is our mother. **27** For it is written,

"REJOICE, BARREN WOMAN WHO DOES NOT BEAR; BREAK FORTH AND SHOUT, YOU WHO ARE NOT IN LABOR; FOR MORE NUMEROUS ARE THE CHILDREN OF THE DESOLATE THAN OF THE ONE WHO HAS A HUSBAND."

28 And you brethren, like Isaac, are children of promise. **29** But as at that time he who was born according to the flesh persecuted him who was born according to the Spirit, so it is now also. **30** But what does the Scripture say?

"CAST OUT THE BONDWOMAN AND HER SON, FOR THE SON OF THE BONDWOMAN SHALL NOT BE AN HEIR WITH THE SON OF THE FREE WOMAN."

31 So then, brethren, we are not children of a bondwoman, but of the free woman.

1 It was for freedom that Christ set us free; therefore keep standing firm and do not be subject again to a yoke of slavery.

2 Behold I, Paul, say to you that if you receive circumcision, Christ will be of no benefit to you. 3 And I testify again to every man who receives circumcision, that he is under obligation to keep the whole Law. 4 You have been severed from Christ, you who are seeking to be justified by law; you have fallen from grace. 5 For we through the Spirit, by faith, are waiting for the hope of righteousness. 6 For in Christ Jesus neither circumcision nor uncircumcision means anything, but faith working through love.

7 You were running well; who hindered you from obeying the truth? 8 This persuasion did not come from Him who calls you. 9 A little leaven leavens the whole lump of dough. 10 I have confidence in you in the Lord that you will adopt no other view; but the one who is disturbing you will bear his judgment, whoever he is. 11 But I, brethren, if I still preach circumcision, why am I still persecuted? Then the stumbling block of the cross has been abolished. 12 I wish that those who are troubling you would even mutilate themselves.

13 For you were called to freedom, brethren; only do not turn your freedom into an opportunity for the flesh, but through love serve one another. 14 For the whole Law is fulfilled in one word, in the statement, "YOU SHALL LOVE YOUR NEIGHBOR AS YOURSELF." 15 But if you bite and devour one another, take care that you are not consumed by one another.

16 But I say, walk by the Spirit, and you will not carry out the desire of the flesh. 17 For

the flesh sets its desire against the Spirit, and the Spirit against the flesh; for these are in opposition to one another, so that you may not do the things that you please. 18 But if you are led by the Spirit, you are not under the Law. 19 Now the deeds of the flesh are evident, which are: immorality, impurity, sensuality, 20 idolatry, sorcery, enmities, strife, jealousy, outbursts of anger, disputes, dissensions, factions, 21 envying, drunkenness, carousing, and things like these, of which I forewarn you, just as I have forewarned you, that those who practice such things will not inherit the kingdom of God. 22 But the fruit of the Spirit is love, joy, peace, patience, kindness, goodness, faithfulness, 23 gentleness, self-control; against such things there is no law. 24 Now those who belong to Christ Jesus have crucified the flesh with its passions and desires.

25 If we live by the Spirit, let us also walk by the Spirit. 26 Let us not become boastful, challenging one another, envying one another.

GALATIANS 6

1 Brethren, even if anyone is caught in any trespass, you who are spiritual, restore such a one in a spirit of gentleness; each one looking to yourself, so that you too will not be tempted. 2 Bear one another's burdens, and thereby fulfill the law of Christ. 3 For if anyone thinks he is something when he is nothing, he deceives himself. 4 But each one must examine his own work, and then he will have reason for boasting in regard to himself alone, and not in regard to another. 5 For each one will bear his own load.

6 The one who is taught the word is to share all good things with the one who teaches him. 7 Do not be deceived, God is not mocked; for whatever a man sows, this he will also reap. 8 For the one who sows to his own flesh will from the flesh reap corruption, but the one who sows to the Spirit will from the Spirit reap eternal life. 9 Let us not lose heart in doing good, for in due time we will reap if we do not grow weary. 10 So then, while we have opportunity, let us do good to all people, and especially to those who are of the household of the faith.

11 See with what large letters I am writing to you with my own hand. 12 Those who desire to make a good showing in the flesh try to compel you to be circumcised, simply so that they will not be persecuted for the cross of Christ. 13 For those who are circumcised do not even keep the Law themselves, but they desire to have you circumcised so that they may boast in your flesh. 14 But may it never be that I would boast, except in the cross of our Lord Jesus Christ, through which the world has been crucified to me, and I to the world. 15 For neither is circumcision anything, nor uncircumcision, but a new creation. 16 And those who will walk by this rule, peace and mercy be upon them, and upon the Israel of God.

17 From now on let no one cause trouble for me, for I bear on my body the brand-marks of Jesus.

18 The grace of our Lord Jesus Christ be with your spirit, brethren. Amen.

WEEK 1: Conversion Then Commitment

Important: Grab your favorite colored pens or pencils!

We will spend time throughout the next six weeks marking various key words in color. Key words bring out themes and important elements in God's Word. If you discover other important words or phrases that emphasize and drive home spiritual lessons, be sure to mark them too.

Using the text at the beginning of the study, read **GALATIANS 1** all the way through two times, praying and asking for sight to see His truths.

- As you read the first time mark **GOD** with a black G.
- The second time you read mark **JESUS CHRIST** with a red cross.

Continually be on the lookout for **God** and **Jesus Christ**, always marking these two words as you read. The presence of **God** and **Jesus Christ** is pivotal in our faith and in our text.

Lesson 1: Mirrors of Distortion

Galatians 1:1-9

1 Paul, an apostle (not sent from men nor through the agency of man, but through Jesus Christ and God the Father, who raised Him from the dead), 2 and all the brethren who are with me, To the churches of Galatia:

3 Grace to you and peace from God our Father and the Lord Jesus Christ, 4 who gave Himself for our sins so that He might rescue us from this present evil age, according to the will of our God and Father, 5 to whom be the glory forevermore. Amen.

6 I am amazed that you are so quickly deserting Him who called you by the grace of Christ, for a different gospel; 7 which is really not another; only there are some who are disturbing you and want to distort the gospel of Christ. 8 But even if we, or an angel from heaven, should preach to you a gospel contrary to what we have preached to you, he is to be accursed! 9 As we have said before, so I say again now, if any man is preaching to you a gospel contrary to what you received, he is to be accursed!

As you walk through each lesson make sure you are sticking to the Word as you think through your answers and the activities.

Let's focus on the first nine verses of Galatians. We can find much as we dig into God's Word today. Get your shovel, roll up your sleeves, and let's begin digging.

Share any knowledge you have about the apostle Paul.

It is amazing to me how a definition can broaden our understanding of a text. According to our text, what is an **apostle**?

Define an **apostle** using a dictionary or the internet (dictionary.com).

Who sent Paul as an apostle?

According to the text, what is the will of our God and Father?

Read **Galatians 1:6-9** in the New Living Translation, noting phrases and words that are different:

"I am shocked that you are turning away so soon from God, who called you to himself through the loving mercy of Christ. You are following a different way that pretends to be the Good News but is not the Good News at all. You are being fooled by those who deliberately twist the truth concerning Christ. Let God's curse fall on anyone, including us or even an angel from heaven, who preaches a different kind of Good News than the one we preached to you. I say again what we have said before: If anyone preaches any other Good News than the one you welcomed, let that person be cursed." *–NLT*

Summarize what you hear Paul saying to the church in Galatia.

Explain Paul's amazement with the Galatians, according to the text.

As you read **Galatians 1:1-9** again, mark **gospel** with a lowercase brown **g**. Marking in color helps the key words stand out. What do you learn from the text about the **gospel** Paul speaks of?

I often think of the county fairs I went to with my friends while in high school. We found the Hall of Distorted Mirrors so fun and entertaining. Think of somewhere in our world where the gospel we know to be true has been distorted, as I was when I stood in front of the mirrors at the fair.

What does Paul say will happen to any man who distorts the truth of the gospel of Christ?

Share why it is important to know Him who called you by the grace of Christ.

 Let's have some fun. Use the letters G-O-S-P-E-L to create phrases or words that describe the meaning of GOSPEL to you.

G

O

S

P

E

L

Lesson 2: Proof Is in the Pudding

Galatians 1:10-12

10 For am I now seeking the favor of men, or of God? Or am I striving to please men? If I were still trying to please men, I would not be a bond-servant of Christ. 11 For I would have you know, brethren, that the gospel which was preached by me is not according to man. 12 For I neither received it from man, nor was I taught it, but I received it through a revelation of Jesus Christ.

List the questions Paul is asking in **Galatians 1:10-12**.

Share a time when you have asked these same questions of yourself.

Rewrite verse 10 below. How is a "bond-servant of Christ" characterized? If you are unsure of what a bond-servant is, take the time to look up a definition or search a concordance for other occurrences of bond-servant in God's Word.

"Bond-servant" appears 25 times in the New American Standard translation of the New Testament. No other translation uses the word bond-servant. Paul is calling himself a bond-servant of Christ. Read **Philippians 2:5-8** below and compare it to **Galatians 1:10**. Whom is Paul speaking to in Philippians and what does he speak of?

> Your attitude should be the same as that of Christ Jesus: Who, being in very nature God, did not consider equality with God something to be grasped, but made himself nothing, taking the very nature of a servant, being made in human likeness. And being found in appearance as a man, he humbled himself and became obedient to death – even death on a cross! –NIV '84

Mark **gospel** in verse 11 with your lowercase brown **g** as you did in verses 1-9.
Record what you learn about the **gospel** from **Galatians 1:10-12**.

Read of Paul's "revelation of Jesus Christ" in **Acts 9:1-9**.

Now Saul, still breathing threats and murder against the disciples of the Lord, went to the high priest, and asked for letters from him to the synagogues at Damascus, so that if he found any belonging to the Way, both men and women, he might bring them bound to Jerusalem. As he was traveling, it happened that he was approaching Damascus, and suddenly a light from heaven flashed around him; and he fell to the ground and heard a voice saying to him, "Saul, Saul, why are you persecuting Me?" And he said, "Who are You, Lord?" And He said, "I am Jesus whom you are persecuting, but get up and enter the city, and it will be told you what you must do." The men who traveled with him stood speechless, hearing the voice but seeing no one. Saul got up from the ground, and though his eyes were open, he could see nothing; and leading him by the hand, they brought him into Damascus. And he was three days without sight, and neither ate nor drank."

What was Paul doing when a light from heaven flashed around him? What was his immediate reaction?

Share what you were doing when God called out your name. What was your response? Was it immediate? Did you ignore him? I have heard it said that we must hear the gospel spoken to us seven times before we choose to believe and accept His truth and love.

I want you to know, brothers, that the gospel I preached is not something that man made up. I did not receive it from any man, nor was I taught it; rather, I received it by revelation from Jesus Christ.
–Galatians 1:11-12, NIV '84

Lesson 3: The Past Is Part of Ur Future

13 For you have heard of my former manner of life in Judaism, how I used to persecute the church of God beyond measure and tried to destroy it; 14 and I was advancing in Judaism beyond many of my contemporaries among my countrymen, being more extremely zealous for my ancestral traditions. 15 But when God, who had set me apart even from my mother's womb and called me through His grace, was pleased 16 to reveal His Son in me so that I might preach Him among the Gentiles, I did not immediately consult with flesh and blood, 17 nor did I go up to Jerusalem to those who were apostles before me; but I went away to Arabia, and returned once more to Damascus.

We all have a past and somehow it plays into our present and our future. Wow, Paul had a past. List all that is part of Paul's past. Refer to **Acts 9** to add details of Paul's past.

Explain God's involvement in Paul's life, according to **Galatians 1:15-16a**.

Paul says he did not immediately consult with flesh and blood, nor did he go up to Jerusalem to those who were apostles before him. What do you hear Paul saying?

Many times in our lives we turn immediately to another for understanding, clarification, or answers when our past collides with our present, or our future is foggy and uncertain. What do you think God is longing for you to do instead? What would His purpose be in asking you to do this?

Why do you think Paul would go away from flesh and blood and those who were apostles before him?

Tell of a time when you have been in the desert spiritually or relationally. What were the results of your time there?

I believe oftentimes we don't spend enough time thinking about where we have been, where God has brought us and where we are supposed to be going. Sketch a diagram, create a timeline, or design an outline using pictures, words, or both of how God has taken your past and is making it part of your future. Please don't rush through this activity. Take time to reflect on **Psalm 139** and **Jeremiah 29:11**.

Lesson 4: Because of Me or God?

Galatians 1:18–24

18 Then three years later I went up to Jerusalem to become acquainted with Cephas, and stayed with him fifteen days. 19 But I did not see any other of the apostles except James, the Lord's brother. 20 (Now in what I am writing to you, I assure you before God that I am not lying.) 21 Then I went into the regions of Syria and Cilicia. 22 I was still unknown by sight to the churches of Judea which were in Christ; 23 but only, they kept hearing, "He who once persecuted us is now preaching the faith which he once tried to destroy." 24 And they were glorifying God because of me.

Reread **Galatians 1:1-17** and note where Paul was.

It's now three years later and Paul is on the move. Let's recreate his travel itinerary and travel companions by sorting through and listing:

The places Paul has traveled:

The people he has seen as he has traveled:

The time periods Paul stayed where he traveled:

Paul speaks of going up to Jerusalem to become acquainted with Cephas, where he stayed for 15 days. According to **John 1:42**, who is Cephas also known as?

> "He immediately led him to Jesus. Jesus took one look up and said, "You're John's son, Simon? From now on your name is Cephas" (or Peter, which means "Rock")." –*The Message*

Acts 9:26 brings us background and insight as to why Paul would spend 15 days with Peter [Cephas]. What does it say?

> "When Saul arrived in Jerusalem, he tried to meet with the believers, but they were all afraid of him. They did not believe he had truly become a believer!" –*NLT*

Can you name the 12 apostles according to **Acts 1:12-26**? Paul has seen Peter [Cephas] and James, the Lord's brother. Whom has he not seen?

Galatians 1:20 seems out of place. Reread **verses 18-24**. What are some reasonable explanations for Paul going to such extremes to assure the Galatians that he is not lying?

Tell about a time when you found yourself in a situation where you needed to convince another that you were telling the truth. Do you recall why this person struggled to believe you?

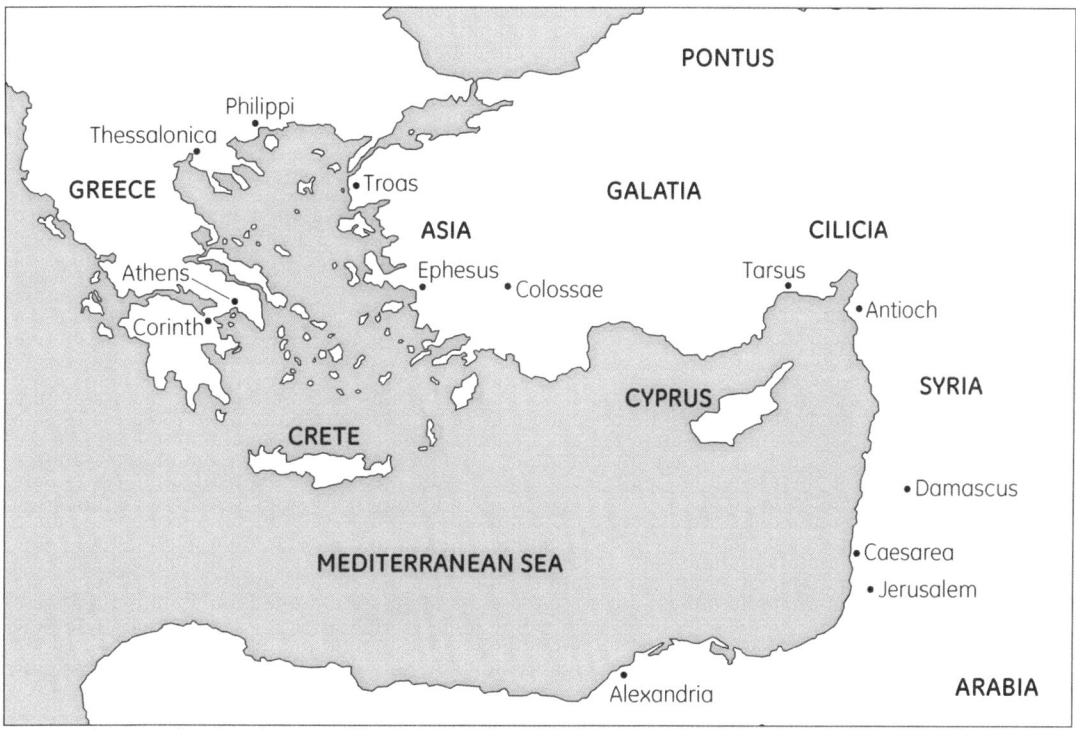

Looking at the map above, gain a sense for Paul's journey as he left Jerusalem. Think about the means of transportation for traveling at that time, the distance, and Paul's stamina. According to the text, what could Paul expect from the churches as he headed into these regions?

Paul is headed where after Jerusalem?

Think about Paul traveling into Syria and Cilicia. He was known to the churches of Judea only by reputation. They chose to believe what they heard. What is it about Paul that causes the churches of Judea to glorify God?

 Identify someone who has caused you to glorify God because of his or her life. Share details about this person's life without sharing who the person is.

Don't Stop Yet . . .

Take some time to go to the beginning of the study where you find the book of **Galatians**. Using your colored pencils and marking symbols, mark the key words again in this section of the study. You marked **God** with a black G, **Jesus Christ** with a red cross, and **gospel** with a lowercase brown g as you worked through **Galatians 1**.

Which verse or verses from **Galatians 1** carry the most meaning for you? Explain why.

Record this on a 3x5 index card and commit it to memory.

Paul shared in **Galatians 1:13-15** of his former manner of life, when God got a hold of him, and his quest forward to speak the gospel. Your conversion may not be as grand as Paul's in Acts 9, but knowing Jesus Christ as your personal Savior gives you a story to tell. Thinking of your past, your present, and the future God is calling you to, take some time to share your story as Paul shared his.

A Note From Lisa

I greet you at the end of this first week with two great words, grace and peace! We know the meaning of those words because Jesus Christ rescued us from this evil world we're in by offering Himself as a sacrifice for our sins. God's plan is that we all experience that rescue. Glory to God forever! Oh, yes! May God faithfully unfold His truths to you as you faithfully study Galatians 2. May the Lord make His face shine upon you and be gracious to you.

Sincerely studying God's Word with you,

Going DEEPER STILL in Week 1

WEEK 2: 2 B or Not 2 B

Read **GALATIANS 1-2**. Then go back and read Galatians 2 again, praying and asking for sight to see His truths.

- As you read Galatians 2, mark **GOD** with a black G.
- As you read Galatians 2 again, mark **JESUS CHRIST** with a red cross.

Continually be on the lookout for **God** and **Jesus Christ**, always marking these two words as you read. The presence of **God** and **Jesus Christ** is pivotal in our faith and in our text.

Lesson 1: The Man for the Job

Galatians 2:1–10

1 Then after an interval of fourteen years I went up again to Jerusalem with Barnabas, taking Titus along also. 2 It was because of a revelation that I went up; and I submitted to them the gospel which I preach among the Gentiles, but I did so in private to those who were of reputation, for fear that I might be running, or had run, in vain. 3 But not even Titus, who was with me, though he was a Greek, was compelled to be circumcised. 4 But it was because of the false brethren secretly brought in, who had sneaked in to spy out our liberty which we have in Christ Jesus, in order to bring us into bondage. 5 But we did not yield in subjection to them for even an hour, so that the truth of the gospel would remain with you. 6 But from those who were of high reputation (what they were makes no difference to me; God shows no partiality)—well, those who were of reputation contributed nothing to me. 7 But on the contrary, seeing that I had been entrusted with the gospel to the uncircumcised, just as Peter had been to the circumcised 8 (for He who effectually worked for Peter in his apostleship to the circumcised effectually worked for me also to the Gentiles), 9 and recognizing the grace that had been given to me, James and Cephas and John, who were reputed to be pillars, gave to me and Barnabas the right hand of fellowship, so that we might go to the Gentiles and they to the circumcised. 10 They only asked us to remember the poor—the very thing I also was eager to do.

As you walk through each lesson make sure you are sticking to the Word as you think through your answers and the activities.

Take with you all you studied in **Galatians 1** as we begin to dig into **Galatians 2**, remembering where Paul had been, why he is writing to the church in Galatia, and where he was physically.

List below all the people Paul mentions in **Galatians 2:1-10** and anything you learn about them.

I find value and clarity in Scripture by using all the different translations we are blessed with. Read **Galatians 2:2** from the New Living Translation and note which phrases or words might be different.

"I went there because God revealed to me that I should go. While I was there I met privately with those considered to be leaders of the church and shared with them the message I had been preaching to the Gentiles. I wanted to make sure that we were in agreement, for fear that all my efforts had been wasted and I was running the race for nothing." –NLT

Why did Paul go to Jerusalem?

Think about these words: "I went because God revealed to me that I should go." I know I have often thought about them. What meaning do they have to you? Have you ever gone because God revealed to you that you should go? Go to the grocery and make a meal for someone? Go to the phone and call a friend who is on your heart? Go to a city and start a new job? Share the details, please. How did you know you were to go? Did you go right away? What did your revelation look like?

With whom does Paul meet privately in Jerusalem, and in hopes of what?

Paul is running a race and is fearful it is all for nothing. In **1 Corinthians 9:24**, what is Paul hoping to win?

"Do you not know that those who run in a race all run, but *only* one receives the prize? Run in such a way that you may win."

We are all running a race, just like Paul. Some are running the race in vain and some are running to receive the prize. Are you running in such a way that you will win? What does this look like to you? How do you run?

Oftentimes you will see contrasts used in God's Word to show differences. In **Galatians 2:2-7** Paul makes many contrasts. Be affirmed that this may be something you have never taken notice of before, but once you have pushed through, you will see more and more contrasts in God's Word as you read. They will bring the Scriptures to life and understanding will come with your perseverance. List each occurrence of "**but**" and see if you can work your way through the contrasts.

We cannot miss all the references to **circumcision** in **Galatians 2**. Travel back through **Galatians 2** marking each **circumcision** with scissors.

Record the verses where **circumcision** appears and what was being said each time.

Nuggets of gold are found throughout **Galatians 2:7-10**. Record who is doing what … to whom … and why.

How would you explain to one with no knowledge of Scripture the "right hand of fellowship" given to Paul and Barnabas? Could you compare it to something from our world?

"**So that**" in Scripture often explains an action. **Galatians 1:4**: "…who gave Himself for our sins *so that* He might rescue us from this present evil age…" If we look at the "**so that**" we see God giving Himself for our sins because He wants to rescue us from this present evil age. "**So that**" plays a very important part in the structure of God's Word.

Look at the verses below and record the reasons given within each situation after the "**so that**."
Rewrite the verse in your own words as I did above, showing you understand the function of "**so that**."

2:5

2:9

As you continue studying Galatians, don't miss the reasons given for many actions taken by Paul and others. Haven't we all said at one time or another, "but why?" We can even find ourselves breathing those words to God. "Mommy, why do I have to go to the dentist? Why do I have to go to the doctor? Why do I have to obey you?" "So that you can live a long and happy life," Mommy answers. Think deeper about these questions. Why do you think little children to grown adults desire to know why?

Have you ever felt like God said, "It's a 'need to know' situation and you don't need to know yet"?
How do you deal with that kind of an answer?

Thank you, Almighty, for always knowing and protecting us when it's not time for us to know. Help us to trust You more and more with each situation we walk through with You. Amen.

Lesson 2: Opposition at Its Best

11 But when Cephas came to Antioch, I opposed him to his face, because he stood condemned. 12 For prior to the coming of certain men from James, he used to eat with the Gentiles; but when they came, he began to withdraw and hold himself aloof, fearing the party of the circumcision. 13 The rest of the Jews joined him in hypocrisy, with the result that even Barnabas was carried away by their hypocrisy. 14 But when I saw that they were not straightforward about the truth of the gospel, I said to Cephas in the presence of all, "If you, being a Jew, live like the Gentiles and not like the Jews, how is it that you compel the Gentiles to live like Jews?

Read **Galatians 2:1-14**. Now, reread **Galatians 2:11-14**. What is the tone you sense as you read?

Why are some people drawn to conflict like the air we breathe, but others run from it?

Where do you fall on the spectrum of conflict? Love it or run from it?

Where do we see Paul on the spectrum of conflict, if **Galatians 2:11-14** is all we have to make a judgment? Support your thoughts.

Maybe if we read **Galatians 2:11-14** in another translation the tone will sound different.

"When Peter came to Antioch, I opposed him to his face, because he was clearly in the wrong. Before certain men came from James, he used to eat with the Gentiles. But when they arrived, he began to draw back and separate himself from the Gentiles because he was afraid of those who belonged to the circumcision group. The other Jews joined him in his hypocrisy, so that by their hypocrisy even Barnabas was led astray. When I saw that they were not acting in line with the truth of the gospel, I said to Peter in front of them all, "You are a Jew, yet you live like a Gentile and not like a Jew. How is it, then, that you force Gentiles to follow Jewish customs?'" *–NIV '84*

Paul still sounds upset. Would you be as bold as Paul in accusing Peter? Why did Paul feel he had the right to speak as he did to Peter?

After reading **2 Corinthians 6:14-18**, bridge the truths found here with the situation between Paul and Peter. Know your audience and look closely at Peter's behavior.

"Do not be bound together with unbelievers; for what partnership have righteousness and lawlessness, or what fellowship has light with darkness? Or what harmony has Christ with Belial, or what has a believer in common with an unbeliever? Or what agreement has the temple of God with idols? For we are the temple of the living God; just as God said, "I WILL DWELL IN THEM AND WALK AMONG THEM; AND I WILL BE THEIR GOD, AND THEY SHALL BE MY PEOPLE. "Therefore, COME OUT FROM THEIR MIDST AND BE SEPARATE," says the Lord. "AND DO NOT TOUCH WHAT IS UNCLEAN; And I will welcome you. 'And I will be a father to you, And you shall be sons and daughters to Me,' says the Lord Almighty."

According to **2 Corinthians 6:14-18** above, what was Peter doing that was so offensive to Paul?

As we run our race of faith in Jesus Christ, pressing toward the prize, it is a wonderful asset to have one who will hold us accountable to the truths of God's Word. What words or phrases come to your mind when you think of accountability?

Share an experience you have had with an accountability partner as you have run your race.

What lessons can you learn from Paul's passion and approach in this situation with Peter?

Lesson 3: Origin of Salvation

Galatians 2:15–21

15 "We are Jews by nature and not sinners from among the Gentiles; **16** nevertheless knowing that a man is not justified by the works of the Law but through faith in Christ Jesus, even we have believed in Christ Jesus, so that we may be justified by faith in Christ and not by the works of the Law; since by the works of the Law no flesh will be justified. **17** "But if, while seeking to be justified in Christ, we ourselves have also been found sinners, is Christ then a minister of sin? May it never be! **18** "For if I rebuild what I have once destroyed, I prove myself to be a transgressor. **19** "For through the Law I died to the Law, so that I might live to God. **20** "I have been crucified with Christ; and it is no longer I who live, but Christ lives in me; and the life which I now live in the flesh I live by faith in the Son of God, who loved me and gave Himself up for me. **21** "I do not nullify the grace of God, for if righteousness comes through the Law, then Christ died needlessly."

Truly, we can never read God's Word too many times. Each time you will see something you didn't see the last time. As you read **Galatians 2:15-21**, mark **Law** with a green open book.

Share below your impressions as you read.

What do you know about the Law that is being spoken of here in **Galatians 2:15-21**?

To bring more depth to the Law Paul speaks of, enjoy digging deeper into the following passages. Record what you see and read, thinking of the who, what, where, when, and why of God's Word.

Matthew 5:17-20

Luke 16:14-17

John 1:14-18

To go DEEPER STILL in your understanding, the entire book of Romans covers the Law. "Law" appears 76 times in the New American Standard version of Romans. I would suggest spending quality quiet time reading Romans from beginning to end. As you dig, ask God for wisdom in understanding the role of the Law in our lives today.

Who are the two groups being talked about in **Galatians 2:15-21**?

What is the main discussion going back and forth?

Have you identified the "**so that**" statements? Record below the action and the reason behind the action in **Galatians 2:16, 19**.

In one word, how would you describe Paul's attitude as he speaks in **Galatians 2:14-21**?

What gives him such confidence in who he is and what he believes? Use the text to support your thoughts.

What justifies a man? What doesn't justify a man?

Define **justify** using a dictionary or dictionary.com.

Paul claims he "died to the Law **so that** he may live to God." Record all evidence from **Galatians 1 and 2** defending this claim.

If you stood before a grand jury, would there be enough evidence to convict you of living unto God? Knowing that we are "not justified by the works of the law but through the faith in Christ Jesus," why should there be evidence of our faith, according to Galatians 2:20? Is it enough?

Don't Stop Yet . . .

Travel back to the beginning of the study where you find the book of **Galatians**. Using your colored pencils and marking symbols, mark your key words from **Galatians 2** in this section of the study. You marked **God** with a black G, **Jesus Christ** with a red cross, **circumcision** with scissors and **Law** with a green open book.

Read **Galatians 1 and 2** with your key word markings. As you read, think about all the questions that have been asked in order to bring you new insight.

Share which verse or verses from **Galatians 2** carry a lesson for your life that you need to give more attention to.

Record this on a 3x5 index card and commit it to memory.

Where in your faith are you experiencing the most difficulty living for God?

For when I tried to keep the law, it condemned me. So I died to the law—I stopped trying to meet all its requirements—so that I might live for God. –*Galatians 2:19, NLT*

Commit this difficulty to God in a written prayer in the space below. Be real and seek His face as you long to no longer live unto yourself but to live wholly unto Christ, the Perfecter and Author of your faith.

"Therefore, since we have so great a cloud of witnesses surrounding us, let us also lay aside every encumbrance and the sin which so easily entangles us, and let us run with endurance the race that is set before us, fixing our eyes on Jesus, the author and perfecter of faith, who for the joy set before Him endured the cross, despising the shame, and has sat down at the right hand of the throne of God. For consider Him who has endured such hostility by sinners against Himself, so that you will not grow weary and lose heart." –*Hebrews 12:1-3*

A Note From Lisa

We have been crucified with Christ and no longer live, but Christ lives in us. The life we live in the body, we live by faith in the Son of God, who loved us and gave himself for us. May God faithfully unfold His truths to you as you faithfully study Galatians 3. May the Lord make His face shine upon you and be gracious to you.

Sincerely studying God's Word with you,

Going DEEPER STILL in Week 2

WEEK 3: Bewitched!

Read **GALATIANS 1-3**. Then go back and read Galatians 3 again, praying and asking for sight to see His truths.

- As you read Galatians 3, mark **GOD** with a black G.
- As you read Galatians 3 again, mark **JESUS CHRIST** with a red cross.

Continually be on the lookout for **God** and **Jesus Christ**, always marking these two words as you read. The presence of **God** and **Jesus Christ** are pivotal in our faith and in our text.

Lesson 1: The Spirit

Galatians 3:1-5

1 You foolish Galatians, who has bewitched you, before whose eyes Jesus Christ was publicly portrayed as crucified? 2 This is the only thing I want to find out from you: did you receive the Spirit by the works of the Law, or by hearing with faith? 3 Are you so foolish? Having begun by the Spirit, are you now being perfected by the flesh? 4 Did you suffer so many things in vain—if indeed it was in vain? 5 So then, does He who provides you with the Spirit and works miracles among you, do it by the works of the Law, or by hearing with faith?

As you walk through each lesson make sure you are sticking to the Word as you think through your answers and the activities.

Let's look back before we move forward. List below one highlight, one key word truth, or one important verse from **Galatians 1 and 2**.

Galatians 1:

Galatians 2:

From **Galatians 3**, write one truth that was familiar to you, a question you have, or a theme that you recognized as soon as you were done reading.

Keeping up with the context of Galatians is so important. This is why we will read, reread, and mark phrases and key words. A deeper understanding of God's Word and Paul's message is my desire for you.

Thinking of key words, let's identify the entrance of **Spirit** in these first five verses with blue wings. Then continue marking **Law** with a green open book in **Galatians 3**. What have you learned about the **Spirit** and the **Law** as you marked? Record the verse these words appeared in and what was being said about each.

Why was Paul so upset that he would call the Galatians "foolish"? He has such a different tone of voice from **Galatians 1:6**.

Although Paul asks four questions in the first five verses of **Galatians 3**, he states there is only one thing he wants to know. What is it? Share why you think this question is pressing on him so heavily. Reread **Galatians 2** for recall if necessary.

Let's go back in time to the show *Bewitched*. Do you remember the characters? The story line? What picture comes to mind as Paul is addressing the Galatians as "foolish" and asking them who has "bewitched" them?

To bewitch means *to cast a spell over, to enchant, or to fascinate*. What have the Galatians become enchanted and fascinated with?

Share a time when you found yourself "bewitched" or enchanted with this world. How did it draw your attention away from "He who provides you with the Spirit and works miracles among you"?

In **Galatians 3:3**, "being perfected by the flesh" is another way of saying what? Think about all you have faithfully studied so far.

Mark **faith** in **Galatians 3:1-5** with a blue upward arrow. You will be surprised how much faith you will find in all of **Galatians 3**. Please take time to record the verse number and what you learned about **faith** from these first five verses.

 **In your experience, what is the hardest part of living by faith and not by works of the Law?**

Paul asks four questions of the Galatians. Underline the four questions in the text and circle the question marks. Then list the four questions below.

1.

2.

3.

4.

"You crazy Galatians! Did someone put a hex on you? Have you taken leave of your senses? Something crazy has happened, for it's obvious that you no longer have the crucified Jesus in clear focus in your lives. His sacrifice on the cross was certainly set before you clearly enough." –*Galatians 3:1, The Message*

Sit with yourself for a moment or two, recalling a time you might have been as upset as Paul and fired questions at your target, giving no time for answers. The answers weren't the important part for Paul; it was getting the questions out in hopes of making the Galatians think! What was the basis for your anger? Paul's is righteous anger. His Galatians are falling away from the gospel He preached to them.

How would you have reacted if you had shared the gospel with friends, watched them come to faith, and you were now watching them walk with the world through "bewitched" eyesight?

"Answer this question: Does the God who lavishly provides you with his own presence, his Holy Spirit, working things in your lives you could never do for yourselves, does he do these things because of your strenuous moral striving or because you trust him to do them in you?" –*Galatians 3:5, The Message*

Lesson 2: U R Redeemed

Galatians 3:6–14

6 Even so Abraham BELIEVED GOD, AND IT WAS RECKONED TO HIM AS RIGHTEOUSNESS. 7 Therefore, be sure that it is those who are of faith who are sons of Abraham. 8 The Scripture, foreseeing that God would justify the Gentiles by faith, preached the gospel beforehand to Abraham, saying, "ALL THE NATIONS WILL BE BLESSED IN YOU." 9 So then those who are of faith are blessed with Abraham, the believer. 10 For as many as are of the works of the Law are under a curse; for it is written, "CURSED IS EVERYONE WHO DOES NOT ABIDE BY ALL THINGS WRITTEN IN THE BOOK OF THE LAW, TO PERFORM THEM." 11 Now that no one is justified by the Law before God is evident; for, "THE RIGHTEOUS MAN SHALL LIVE BY FAITH." 12 However, the Law is not of faith; on the contrary, "HE WHO PRACTICES THEM SHALL LIVE BY THEM." 13 Christ redeemed us from the curse of the Law, having become a curse for us—for it is written, "CURSED IS EVERYONE WHO HANGS ON A TREE"— 14 in order that in Christ Jesus the blessing of Abraham might come to the Gentiles, so that we would receive the promise of the Spirit through faith.

Let's continue marking **Law** and **faith** as we see them here in verses 6-14. Record what you learn about **Law** and **faith** from **Galatians 3:6-14**.

Recording what you learn about what you have marked begins to bring understanding through your discipline of observation. We are striving to learn from observing what God's Word is speaking to us. Remember to record the verse as you record what you learn about the words.

Whenever there is a "therefore," we must train ourselves to ask what the "therefore" is there for.

What is the "**therefore**" there for in **Galatians 3:7**? Paying close attention and not breezing right over these important words will help you learn to read with meaning. Go ahead and mark it with a green triangle right on top of the word.

"Justified by faith" is a term Christians toss around, but the term oftentimes leaves some perplexed, and perhaps not brave enough to ask what it means. Think about the meaning of justify and the meaning of faith. If you wish to go one step further and jot down a working definition, go for it.

Justify:

Faith:

Put those two meanings together to see if you can formulate a thought as to what the Scriptures meant when it was said that "God would justify the Gentiles by faith" in **Galatians 3:8**.

Why do you believe Abraham's belief in God was "reckoned to him as righteousness"? As you begin to think through this question, let's define some key terms:

Reckon:

Righteousness:

Continuing to reason through Abraham's belief in God being reckoned to him as righteousness, read the following passages, recording what you gather regarding Abraham's faith:

Hebrews 11:8-12, 17-19

Romans 4:1-12

Can you have Abraham's faith as your own? How?

Deeper Still   **Walk through your day. Where are you called to live by faith as you continually grow into a woman of God?**

In **Galatians 3:10-13** we see "**curse(d)**" five times. Mark "**curse(d)**" with a black capital **C**. Then in **Galatians 3:14** we see a **promise**. Mark this **promise** with a purple capital **P**.

Who is being cursed and why? What is the promise and who is it for? Reminder: Stay within the text when answering these questions.

"All who rely on observing the law are under a curse, for it is written: "Cursed is everyone who does not continue to do everything written in the Book of the Law." Clearly no one is justified before God by the law, because, "The righteous will live by faith." The law is not based on faith; on the contrary, "The man who does these things will live by them." Christ redeemed us from the curse of the law by becoming a curse for us, for it is written: "Cursed is everyone who is hung on a tree." *–Galatians 3:10–13, NIV '84*

"**However**" introduces a contrast, a marked difference. In reading **Galatians 3:10-12**, explain what is being contrasted. Read slowly, and think about the key words you have marked. Observing God's Word and beginning to interpret its meaning will bring a lesson for your life. Walk through these steps and embrace all God wants to speak to your heart and into your life.

Four Old Testament phrases are in our New Testament passage. Using your resources, may I challenge you to find out where these four Old Testament phrases come from?

V10:

V11:

V12:

V13:

List situations in daily life in which you hear "redeem," "redeemed," or "redemption." In what context are you hearing these words and what action is taking place? I first think of coupons and Kroger.

Jesus Christ redeemed us. He paid off our debt, cleared our record, with His life. We are no longer under the "curse of the Law" because He became a curse for us. Praise the name of Jesus!

Lesson 3: True Promises

Galatians 3:15–23

15 Brethren, I speak in terms of human relations: even though it is only a man's covenant, yet when it has been ratified, no one sets it aside or adds conditions to it. 16 Now the promises were spoken to Abraham and to his seed. He does not say, "And to seeds," as referring to many, but rather to one, "And to your seed," that is, Christ. 17 What I am saying is this: the Law, which came four hundred and thirty years later, does not invalidate a covenant previously ratified by God, so as to nullify the promise. 18 For if the inheritance is based on law, it is no longer based on a promise; but God has granted it to Abraham by means of a promise. 19 Why the Law then? It was added because of transgressions, having been ordained through angels by the agency of a mediator, until the seed would come to whom the promise had been made. 20 Now a mediator is not for one party only; whereas God is only one. 21 Is the Law then contrary to the promises of God? May it never be! For if a law had been given which was able to impart life, then righteousness would indeed have been based on law. 22 But the Scripture has shut up everyone under sin, so that the promise by faith in Jesus Christ might be given to those who believe. 23 But before faith came, we were kept in custody under the law, being shut up to the faith which was later to be revealed.

Continue marking **Law** with an open green book, **faith** with a blue upward arrow, and **promise** with a purple capital P as you read **Galatians 3:15-23**.

Yes, there are many word markings. **Galatians 3** may prove to be the most challenging of all the weeks we spend together. Be patient, slow down, and enjoy the words of God's Word. They have transforming power.

Staying within the text, what do you hear Paul saying his purpose is?

Consider differences between…**THE COVENANT**…**THE LAW**…**THE PROMISES**, while paying close attention to the contrasts, the **buts**, happening in **Galatians 3:16, 18, 22** and **23**. This will take some effort. I hope you are willing to give it a try. The reward will be worth it.

3:16

3:18

3:22

3:23

Consider to whom these promises were spoken and by whom. Record your thoughts.

What does **Romans 4:13-17** offer additionally about these promises that are so important to our faith?

Words are astounding! **INVALIDATE**…**RATIFY**…**NULLIFY**! And all in one verse! The words can be the exact reason many shy away from studying God's Word without someone to walk them through and tell them their thoughts. Have no fear! Truly you can do this!

Ratify means to confirm by expressing consent or approval.
Nullify means to render legally void.
Invalidate means to discredit.

Rewrite **Galatians 3:17** using these definitions. Take it slowly and think about the text with the definitions in direct relation to the Law, the covenant, and the promises.

Galatians 3 is a fully-loaded shopping cart of goodies! Goodness! May your endurance be strong as we continue to press through all the truths within, pulling out application for our lives.

It would be a fun experience to walk through all of Galatians and record only the questions Paul asks of the believers. He is a question kind of a guy! For now, though, let's examine just the two Paul asks in **Galatians 3**. Write the questions and record his answers.

Reading various translations of the same passage can show differences in word usage, structure, and phrasing. As you read both translations below, note differences between the New American Standard and the New Living Translation for **Galatians 3:19-23**.

19 Why the Law then? It was added because of transgressions, having been ordained through angels by the agency of a mediator, until the seed would come to whom the promise had been made. 20 Now a mediator is not for one party only; whereas God is only one. 21 Is the Law then contrary to the promises of God? May it never be! For if a law had been given which was able to impart life, then righteousness would indeed have been based on law. 22 But the Scripture has shut up everyone under sin, so that the promise by faith in Jesus Christ might be given to those who believe. 23 But before faith came, we were kept in custody under the law, being shut up to the faith which was later to be revealed. –NASB

19 Why, then, was the law given? It was given alongside the promise to show people their sins. But the law was designed to last only until the coming of the child who was promised. God gave his law through angels to Moses, who was the mediator between God and the people. 20 Now a mediator is helpful if more than one party must reach an agreement. But God, who is one, did not use a mediator when he gave his promise to Abraham. 21 Is there a conflict, then, between God's law and God's promises? Absolutely not! If the law could give us new life, we could be made right with God by obeying it. 22 But the Scriptures declare that we are all prisoners of sin, so we receive God's promise of freedom only by believing in Jesus Christ. 23 Before the way of faith in Christ was available to us, we were placed under guard by the law. We were kept in protective custody, so to speak, until the way of faith was revealed. –NLT

Lesson 4: _____ << U Name This Lesson!

> **Galatians 3:24–29**
>
> **24** Therefore the Law has become our tutor to lead us to Christ, so that we may be justified by faith. **25** But now that faith has come, we are no longer under a tutor. **26** For you are all sons of God through faith in Christ Jesus. **27** For all of you who were baptized into Christ have clothed yourselves with Christ. **28** There is neither Jew nor Greek, there is neither slave nor free man, there is neither male nor female; for you are all one in Christ Jesus. **29** And if you belong to Christ, then you are Abraham's descendants, heirs according to promise.

Here we are, the last lesson for chapter 3. Are you rejoicing? Can you go one more mile? Please, go one more mile with me to see the finished truths of Galatians 3.

Mark **faith** and **promise** as you have been marking. Record what you saw as you read and marked these two key words.

Let's observe some key words and phrases we have touched on in Week 1 and 2:

V24   What is the "**therefore**" there for?

Place a square around "**so that**" and share what it explains further.

V25   "**But**" provides us with a contrast. What contrast is being discussed?

59

V28   Paul makes a list using …**nor**…**nor**. What is his purpose in making this list?

V29   "**if**…**then**…" means if the first happens then the second will happen.
            What do you see happening?

That's a great way to observe a passage of Scripture. Let's bring understanding to what you observed and see the application for your life.

"And all who have been united with Christ in baptism have put on Christ, like putting on new clothes." –*Galatians 3:27, NLT*

Think about glancing in God's mirror as you have clothed yourself with Christ. Spiritually, do you dress in the dark? Are you aware of what you're putting on? What do you hope to see when you glance in God's mirror each morning before you begin your day?

Ephesians 4:17-24 speaks of our spiritual wardrobe. Rewrite verse 24 below.

Finally, ponder what you feel is the main message from **Galatians 3:24-29** and create a title to record on the line at the beginning of the lesson.

Don't Stop Yet . . .

Once again, I would love to have you turn to the front of the study to record all your markings from **Galatians 3**. You marked **God** with a black G, **Jesus Christ** with a red cross, **faith** with a blue upwards arrow, **Law** with a green open book, **promise** with a purple capital P, and finally **curse** with a black capital C.

That's a lot of marking, no doubt. You may even be teetering towards annoyance with so much marking. If you will keep an open mind and heart towards the value of God's words, I believe you will be blessed in all your reading of God's Word. The eyes of your heart will surely be enlightened to deeper truths waiting for your observation and interpretation. This will bring transformation to your faith.

Choose one of these key words and reflect on its significance in **Galatians 3**. What important truth would be lost if this key word were not included?

Now choose a verse in which this word appears to commit to memory. Write it below and find it in one other translation as well, possibly the New Living Translation or The Message.

As best as you can, illustrate using pictures what this verse is saying to you.

Committing to memory God's Word will bring transformation to our hearts, minds, and souls. We are not to be of this world. We are of a different world. God's Word should guide our steps and direct our paths as we navigate through this world. Put it into your heart, treasure the depth of the meaning in your mind, and long for application to your life!

A Note From Lisa

What an amazing thought: "We are all daughters of the King through faith in Christ Jesus, for all of us who were baptized into Christ have clothed ourselves with Christ. There is neither Jew nor Greek, slave nor free, male nor female, for we are all one in Christ Jesus. If we belong to Christ, then we are Abraham's seed, and heirs according to the promise." I think of the hymn, "Joint heirs with Jesus as we travel this side, we're a part of the family of God." May God faithfully unfold His truths to you as you faithfully study Galatians 4. May the Lord make His face shine upon you and be gracious to you.

Sincerely studying God's Word with you,

Going DEEPER STILL in Week 3

WEEK 4: Freedom Wins Again and Again

Read **GALATIANS 1-4**. Then go back and read Galatians 4 again, praying and asking for sight to see His truths.

- As you read Galatians 4, mark **GOD** with a black G.
- As you read Galatians 4 again, mark **JESUS CHRIST** with a red cross.

Continually be on the lookout for **God** and **Jesus Christ**, always marking these two words as you read. The presence of **God** and **Jesus Christ** are pivotal in our faith and in our text.

Lesson 1: All in the Family

We are past the halfway mark in our study of Galatians. Congratulations, friend! I want to encourage you to keep pushing yourself to study in new ways, dig deeper, and seek God's truths from God's Word.

Galatians 4:1-7

1 Now I say, as long as the heir is a child, he does not differ at all from a slave although he is owner of everything, 2 but he is under guardians and managers until the date set by the father. 3 So also we, while we were children, were held in bondage under the elemental things of the world. 4 But when the fullness of the time came, God sent forth His Son, born of a woman, born under the Law, 5 so that He might redeem those who were under the Law, that we might receive the adoption as sons. 6 Because you are sons, God has sent forth the Spirit of His Son into our hearts, crying, "Abba! Father!" 7 Therefore you are no longer a slave, but a son; and if a son, then an heir through God.

As you walk through each lesson make sure you are sticking to the Word as you think through your answers and the activities.

Rewriting another's words is a great way to begin comprehending what is being said. Paraphrase what you read in **Galatians 4:1-7**.

Focusing on key words in the text will bring life to it. As you read through **Galatians 4:1-7**, mark **but** and **so that** by placing a square around them. Mark **therefore** with a green triangle right on the word.

Record below what is surrounding these words, asking yourself questions as you search for meaning from the text. Note the verse where the key words and phrases are found.

- What is being contrasted?
- What is being explained?

- What reason is being given?
- What is the "therefore" there for?

Read both **Galatians 3:26-29** and **Galatians 4:1-7**.

3:26 For you are all sons of God through faith in Christ Jesus. **27** For all of you who were baptized into Christ have clothed yourselves with Christ. **28** There is neither Jew nor Greek, there is neither slave nor free man, there is neither male nor female; for you are all one in Christ Jesus. **29** And if you belong to Christ, then you are Abraham's descendants, heirs according to promise.

4:1 Now I say, as long as the heir is a child, he does not differ at all from a slave although he is owner of everything, **2** but he is under guardians and managers until the date set by the father. **3** So also we, while we were children, were held in bondage under the elemental things of the world. **4** But when the fullness of the time came, God sent forth His Son, born of a woman, born under the Law, **5** so that He might redeem those who were under the Law, that we might receive the adoption as sons. **6** Because you are sons, God has sent forth the Spirit of His Son into our hearts, crying, "Abba! Father!" **7** Therefore you are no longer a slave, but a son; and if a son, then an heir through God.

Why do you think Paul feels there is no difference between a slave and an heir as a child?

After examining **Galatians 4:1-7**, why did God send forth His Son?

Adoption is to legally and formally declare that someone who is not one's own child is to be treated and cared for as one's own child – including complete rights of inheritance. According to **Ephesians 1:13-14**, what do we know to be true about our adoption into God's family?

> "And now you Gentiles have also heard the truth, the Good News that God saves you. And when you believed in Christ, he identified you as his own by giving you the Holy Spirit, whom he promised long ago. The Spirit is God's guarantee that he will give us the inheritance he promised and that he has purchased us to be his own people. He did this so we would praise and glorify him." –*NLT*

 **Adoption is all around us, overseas and locally. Share a success story you are familiar with. How did both parties benefit from the adoption, emotionally and relationally?**

Identify similarities with your adoption into God's family. When we become His children, what does he send forth into our hearts?

This is the same Spirit that raised God's Son from the dead, and God has sent Him forth into our hearts. Wow! How can this knowledge impact your day through your thoughts, words, and actions?

Look up **Romans 8:11** and rewrite it in your own words. Be sure to identify which translation you read. Then illustrate it with pictures that pull out the main message.

Think about being a son of the eternal God vs. being a slave to the Law. Sort through the text and list all you read about being a son vs. being a slave.

SON   vs.   SLAVE

What in this world holds you a slave? How is it affecting your relationship with your Abba, your heavenly Father?

"Because you are sons, God has sent forth the Spirit of His Son into your heart!" You no longer need to live as a slave in bondage. Through Jesus Christ, you have been set free. The Galatians heard Paul's message, the gospel, and they knew of Jesus Christ's saving power. Do you know of Jesus Christ's saving power? Share how you know His power. Is it through knowledge or experience, your own or someone else's?

"But when the fullness of the time came, God sent forth His Son, born of a woman, born under the Law, so that He might redeem those who were under the Law, that we might receive the adoption as sons. Because you are sons, God has sent forth the Spirit of His Son into our hearts, crying, "Abba! Father!" Therefore you are no longer a slave, but a son; and if a son, then an heir through God." –Galatians 4:4–7

Lesson 2: All 4 Nothing?

Galatians 4:8-11

8 However at that time, when you did not know God, you were slaves to those which by nature are no gods. 9 But now that you have come to know God, or rather to be known by God, how is it that you turn back again to the weak and worthless elemental things, to which you desire to be enslaved all over again? 10 You observe days and months and seasons and years. 11 I fear for you, that perhaps I have labored over you in vain.

As you read the above verses, mark **know(n)** with an orange capital K. Be sure to record below what you learned as you marked.

What would you say is the difference between knowing God and being known by God?

Paul is expressing a definite attitude so far in **Galatians 4**. What attitude do you hear from Paul? Support your answers with the text.

Paul asks a question of the Galatians that we would all do well to ask of ourselves on a regular basis. Record the question below and then, if possible, personalize it and ask it of yourself.

Interesting! Examine **Galatians 4:9** from the New Living Translation as you consider Paul's question.

> "So now that you know God (or should I say, now that God knows you), why do you want to go back again and become slaves once more to the weak and useless spiritual principles of this world?" *–NLT*

List some of the "weak and useless spiritual principles of this world."

In **Galatians 4:11**, Paul expresses genuine fear. Fear of what?

The Galatians are trying to earn favor with God by observing certain days, months, seasons, and years. Are you catching the general theme yet of Paul's letter to the Galatians? Thinking about this theme, what reason would Paul have to think he is laboring over them in vain?

It's true. If we think long and hard, a person will come to mind whom we too feel we have labored over in vain. It may even be that someone feels he or she has labored in vain over us. Record what you find in **1 Thessalonians 3:5**: (site translation used)

Articulate as best as you can what it means for Paul to have labored in vain over the Galatians. His heart is feeling what?

What do you do when you experience this fear as Paul did? In whose life are you investing, watching them grow in Christ? If there is no one, you may not be able to relate to Paul's fear. If there is no one, you may need to ask yourself why not.

Lesson 3: _____   << U Name This Lesson!

Galatians 4:12–20

12 I beg of you, brethren, become as I am, for I also have become as you are. You have done me no wrong; 13 but you know that it was because of a bodily illness that I preached the gospel to you the first time; 14 and that which was a trial to you in my bodily condition you did not despise or loathe, but you received me as an angel of God, as Christ Jesus Himself. 15 Where then is that sense of blessing you had? For I bear you witness that, if possible, you would have plucked out your eyes and given them to me. 16 So have I become your enemy by telling you the truth? 17 They eagerly seek you, not commendably, but they wish to shut you out so that you will seek them. 18 But it is good always to be eagerly sought in a commendable manner, and not only when I am present with you. 19 My children, with whom I am again in labor until Christ is formed in you— 20 but I could wish to be present with you now and to change my tone, for I am perplexed about you.

As you read **Galatians 4:12-20**, circle all words describing how Paul felt and underline questions asked by Paul. Make a list of the feeling words or phrases and the questions asked.

This is a very emotional selection of verses. Paul is begging at the beginning and ends with being perplexed. Identify what you hear Paul saying to those who are so important to him about their past together, their relationship.

Whom is Paul talking about in **Galatians 4:17**? Who is the "they"? Go back as far in Galatians as you need to. What is their objective in seeking the Galatians?

How would you define **commendable**, based on **Galatians 4:18**?

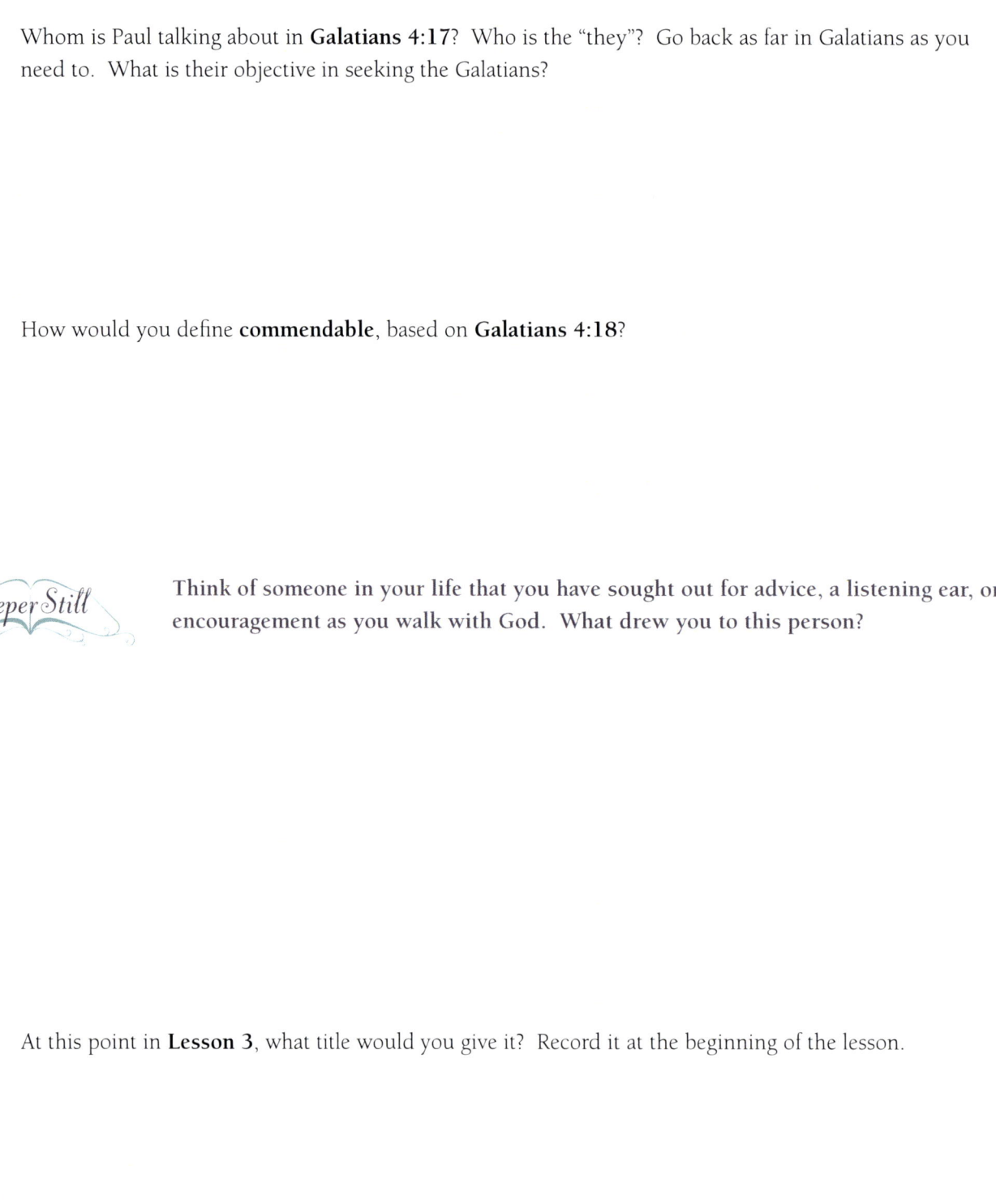

Deeper Still

Think of someone in your life that you have sought out for advice, a listening ear, or encouragement as you walk with God. What drew you to this person?

At this point in **Lesson 3**, what title would you give it? Record it at the beginning of the lesson.

Let's take one last look at this section of Scripture. Compare what you see in the NLT with what is in the NASB. Do you draw different conclusions from the text? Does it shed light upon your understanding?

12 I beg of you, brethren, become as I am, for I also have become as you are. You have done me no wrong; 13 but you know that it was because of a bodily illness that I preached the gospel to you the first time; 14 and that which was a trial to you in my bodily condition you did not despise or loathe, but you received me as an angel of God, as Christ Jesus Himself. 15 Where then is that sense of blessing you had? For I bear you witness that, if possible, you would have plucked out your eyes and given them to me. 16 So have I become your enemy by telling you the truth? 17 They eagerly seek you, not commendably, but they wish to shut you out so that you will seek them. 18 But it is good always to be eagerly sought in a commendable manner, and not only when I am present with you. 19 My children, with whom I am again in labor until Christ is formed in you – 20 but I could wish to be present with you now and to change my tone, for I am perplexed about you. –NASB

12 Dear brothers and sisters, I plead with you to live as I do in freedom from these things, for I have become like you Gentiles—free from those laws. You did not mistreat me when I first preached to you. 13 Surely you remember that I was sick when I first brought you the Good News. 14 But even though my condition tempted you to reject me, you did not despise me or turn me away. No, you took me in and cared for me as though I were an angel from God or even Christ Jesus himself. 15 Where is that joyful and grateful spirit you felt then? I am sure you would have taken out your own eyes and given them to me if it had been possible. 16 Have I now become your enemy because I am telling you the truth? 17 Those false teachers are so eager to win your favor, but their intentions are not good. They are trying to shut you off from me so that you will pay attention only to them. 18 If someone is eager to do good things for you, that's all right; but let them do it all the time, not just when I'm with you. 19 Oh, my dear children! I feel as if I'm going through labor pains for you again, and they will continue until Christ is fully developed in your lives. 20 I wish I were with you right now so I could change my tone. But at this distance I don't know how else to help you. –NLT

Remember, Scripture will interpret Scripture if we are diligent to use our cross-references and dig a little. Pay close attention to the phrases and key words that are slightly different. Is the message different from one translation to another? What differences can you note and write down?

Share a time you became an enemy to another because you told the truth as Paul was bold enough to do. This world is not our home; we are aliens in a strange land. Many are walking both sides of the fence. Maybe you can share a time instead when you were told the truth and someone became your enemy because this person dared speak so boldly to you.

Lesson 4: All About Freedom

Galatians 4:21-31

21 Tell me, you who want to be under law, do you not listen to the law? 22 For it is written that Abraham had two sons, one by the bondwoman and one by the free woman. 23 But the son by the bondwoman was born according to the flesh, and the son by the free woman through the promise. 24 This is allegorically speaking, for these women are two covenants: one proceeding from Mount Sinai bearing children who are to be slaves; she is Hagar. 25 Now this Hagar is Mount Sinai in Arabia and corresponds to the present Jerusalem, for she is in slavery with her children. 26 But the Jerusalem above is free; she is our mother. 27 For it is written, "REJOICE, BARREN WOMAN WHO DOES NOT BEAR; BREAK FORTH AND SHOUT, YOU WHO ARE NOT IN LABOR; FOR MORE NUMEROUS ARE THE CHILDREN OF THE DESOLATE THAN OF THE ONE WHO HAS A HUSBAND." 28 And you brethren, like Isaac, are children of promise. 29 But as at that time he who was born according to the flesh persecuted him who was born according to the Spirit, so it is now also. 30 But what does the Scripture say? "CAST OUT THE BONDWOMAN AND HER SON, FOR THE SON OF THE BONDWOMAN SHALL NOT BE AN HEIR WITH THE SON OF THE FREE WOMAN." 31 So then, brethren, we are not children of a bondwoman, but of the free woman.

Read all of **Galatians 4** as we come to the end of the chapter, pondering the tone and meaning conveyed through Paul's words.

Mark **free** with a circled capital F every time it occurs in **Galatians 4:21-31**.

Mark the contrasts seen throughout this section of Scripture by placing a square around the **but** and then underlining the two elements being contrasted.

4:23

4:26

4:29

4:31

What did you learn from these contrasts?

Paul uses a family situation from the Old Testament to help us understand the struggle between freedom and bondage occurring in the New Testament. Read **Genesis 21:9** for the actual account of Hagar and Sarah's sons.

Travel back to **Galatians 3:29**. Write this verse in the space provided. Make a connection with **Galatians 4:21-31**.

"It wasn't Abraham's sperm that gave identity here, but God's promise. Remember how it was put: 'Your family will be defined by Isaac'? That means that Israelite identity was never racially determined by sexual transmission, but it was God-determined by promise. Remember that promise, 'When I come back next year at this time, Sarah will have a son'?" *–Romans 9:7–9, The Message*

What do you recall about the promise God made to Abraham? How would you find more details about this promise?

Make a collection of words from **Galatians 4:21-31** that holds hope for you. Be creative if you dare by using color and varying word arrangement and size for fun!

God's Word offers all of us hope. Paul's message to the Galatians is one of hope. Paul's message is one of hope for us as well. We have hope because we are children of the free woman! What does freedom feel like to you? Look like? Sound like? What is freedom to you, this freedom Paul speaks of?

Don't Stop Yet . . .

Without looking back at **Galatians 4**, what do you remember from your days of studying God's Word?

What key words do you remember marking? What stands out about these words from **Galatians 4**?

Turning to the front of our study, mark all the key words from your four lessons in **Galatians 4**. You marked **God** with a black G, **Jesus Christ** with a red cross, **know(n)** with an orange capital K, and **free** with a circled capital F.

Select one verse or phrase from this week's lesson you would like to commit to memory and write it below.

Why was this your choice? Transfer this verse or phrase to a 3x5 index card for easy access.

Share a connection you were able to make to your personal life as you studied God's Word this week.

A Note From Lisa

We are free! Praise God we are free! When the time had fully come, God sent his Son, born of a woman, born under law, to redeem us that we might receive the full rights of His daughters. May God faithfully unfold His truths to you as you faithfully study Galatians 5. May the Lord make His face shine upon you and be gracious to you.

Sincerely studying God's Word with you,

Going DEEPER STILL in Week 4

WEEK 5: U R Called . . . to What?

Read **GALATIANS 1-5**. Then go back and read Galatians 5 again, praying and asking for sight to see His truths.

- As you read Galatians 5, mark **GOD** with a black G.
- As you read Galatians 5 again, mark **JESUS CHRIST** with a red cross.

Continually be on the lookout for **God** and **Jesus Christ**, always marking these two words as you read. The presence of **God** and **Jesus Christ** are pivotal in our faith and in our text.

Lesson 1: Firm

Galatians 5:1-6

1 It was for freedom that Christ set us free; therefore keep standing firm and do not be subject again to a yoke of slavery. 2 Behold I, Paul, say to you that if you receive circumcision, Christ will be of no benefit to you. 3 And I testify again to every man who receives circumcision, that he is under obligation to keep the whole Law. 4 You have been severed from Christ, you who are seeking to be justified by law; you have fallen from grace. 5 For we through the Spirit, by faith, are waiting for the hope of righteousness. 6 For in Christ Jesus neither circumcision nor uncircumcision means anything, but faith working through love.

As you walk through each lesson make sure you are sticking to the Word as you think through your answers and the activities.

Mark **circumcision** with scissors and **Spirit** with blue wings as you read **Galatians 5:1-6**.

What knowledge do you have regarding circumcision in the Bible? Write it all down.

Now take that knowledge and couple it with the three occurrences of circumcision in **Galatians 5:1-6**. What connections can be made?

Why did Christ set us free? What have we been set free from?

Only one thing has meaning in Christ Jesus. What is it, according to Paul?

Deeper Still   **Describe what faith expressing itself through love looks like in your day-to-day tasks. Be as detailed as you can.**

In your life what are some issues on which you choose to stand firm and not waver?

Where did your passion for standing firm originate?

It is important for us to understand Paul's message regarding circumcision and the Law. What does he long for the church in Galatia to know and understand?

All of us struggle to resolve the faith versus works question. Share how you came to understand how faith and works fit together. Which comes first? How have you worked it out in your own heart and mind?

Look up each Scripture below and record your findings, along with the translation you used.

Ephesians 2:8-9

Colossians 3:23

James 2:18-22

Make connections for each verse and the section of **Galatians 5** we are studying.

Answer each question. Then match each verse from the previous page with one of the questions below.

What does FAITH look like when it is being lived out?

What do WORKS look like when they are being done without FAITH?

How does one bring together a life of FAITH and WORKS?

"For in Christ Jesus neither circumcision nor uncircumcision means anything but faith working through love." *–Galatians 5:6*

Lesson 2:

<< U Name This Lesson!

Galatians 5:7–15

7 You were running well; who hindered you from obeying the truth? 8 This persuasion did not come from Him who calls you. 9 A little leaven leavens the whole lump of dough. 10 I have confidence in you in the Lord that you will adopt no other view; but the one who is disturbing you will bear his judgment, whoever he is. 11 But I, brethren, if I still preach circumcision, why am I still persecuted? Then the stumbling block of the cross has been abolished. 12 I wish that those who are troubling you would even mutilate themselves. 13 For you were called to freedom, brethren; only do not turn your freedom into an opportunity for the flesh, but through love serve one another. 14 For the whole Law is fulfilled in one word, in the statement, "YOU SHALL LOVE YOUR NEIGHBOR AS YOURSELF." 15 But if you bite and devour one another, take care that you are not consumed by one another.

What are the first four words of this section of Scripture?

Stop and think about that phrase. Read **Hebrews 12:1-2**. Join Paul's words in Hebrews to the first four words here in **Galatians 5:7**.

Pray and seek God regarding your race to the finish. How are you doing? Are you running well? Were you running well? Do you know how to run well? Could you be running better?

As you read **Galatians 5:7-15**, circle the question marks and underline the questions. Record the two questions Paul asks the Galatians.

1.

2.

Imagine you were part of the church in Galatia. How would you have answered Paul's first question?

Mark **circumcision** in **Galatians 5:11**, thinking about the possibilities of why preaching circumcision would lessen Paul's persecution. Consider why circumcision was such a hot topic. Share your thoughts.

Within nine verses we cover running the race well, persecution for preaching circumcision, and a whole lump of dough and a little leaven. Multi-tasking is definitely needed for **Galatians 5:7-15**.

List experiences you have had with leaven and any knowledge you have of its function in recipes.

If you have time to dabble with Google, type in "Functions of Yeast in Baking." See if it takes you to www.dakotayeast.com. "Yeast is a key ingredient and serves three primary functions." Very interesting! The three primary functions of yeast are what? Do you see a connection to Paul's message?

State Paul's purpose for painting this word picture for us: *"A little yeast spreads through the whole batch of dough."* (God's Word)

"It is absolutely clear that God has called you to a free life. Just make sure that you don't use this freedom as an excuse to do whatever you want to do and destroy your freedom. Rather, use your freedom to serve one another in love; that's how freedom grows." *–Galatians 5:13, The Message*

We have been called to freedom! Praise God! What should we be doing with this freedom we are called to?

We are not to do what with our freedom?

We have much to learn about our calling to freedom. Read the following verses and share below what you learned about what you were called to. Think about your freedom in relation to your calling.

Galatians 1:6

Galatians 1:15

Romans 8:28

1 Corinthians 1:9

Deeper Still

Express why it is easier to love ourselves more than our neighbors.

How would you teach 7-year-olds, second graders, to love their neighbor as they love themselves?

After reading both translations of **Galatians 5:7-15** below, highlight similarities and underline differences between phrases and key words.

7 You were running well; who hindered you from obeying the truth? 8 This persuasion did not come from Him who calls you. 9 A little leaven leavens the whole lump of dough. 10 I have confidence in you in the Lord that you will adopt no other view; but the one who is disturbing you will bear his judgment, whoever he is. 11 But I, brethren, if I still preach circumcision, why am I still persecuted? Then the stumbling block of the cross has been abolished. 12 I wish that those who are troubling you would even mutilate themselves. 13 For you were called to freedom, brethren; only do not turn your freedom into an opportunity for the flesh, but through love serve one another. 14 For the whole Law is fulfilled in one word, in the statement, "YOU SHALL LOVE YOUR NEIGHBOR AS YOURSELF." 15 But if you bite and devour one another, take care that you are not consumed by one another.

7 You were running the race so well. Who has held you back from following the truth? 8 It certainly isn't God, for he is the one who called you to freedom. 9 This false teaching is like a little yeast that spreads through the whole batch of dough! 10 I am trusting the Lord to keep you from believing false teachings. God will judge that person, whoever he is, who has been confusing you. 11 Dear brothers and sisters, if I were still preaching that you must be circumcised—as some say I do—why am I still being persecuted? If I were no longer preaching salvation through the cross of Christ, no one would be offended. 12 I just wish that those troublemakers who want to mutilate you by circumcision would mutilate themselves. 13 For you have been called to live in freedom, my brothers and sisters. But don't use your freedom to satisfy your sinful nature. Instead, use your freedom to serve one another in love. 14 For the whole law can be summed up in this one command: "Love your neighbor as yourself." 15 But if you are always biting and devouring one another, watch out! Beware of destroying one another.

Finally, create your own section title for **Galatians 5:7-15** and record it on the line at the beginning of this lesson.

Lesson 3: Set in Motion

Galatians 5:16-26

16 But I say, walk by the Spirit, and you will not carry out the desire of the flesh. **17** For the flesh sets its desire against the Spirit, and the Spirit against the flesh; for these are in opposition to one another, so that you may not do the things that you please. **18** But if you are led by the Spirit, you are not under the Law. **19** Now the deeds of the flesh are evident, which are: immorality, impurity, sensuality, **20** idolatry, sorcery, enmities, strife, jealousy, outbursts of anger, disputes, dissensions, factions, **21** envying, drunkenness, carousing, and things like these, of which I forewarn you, just as I have forewarned you, that those who practice such things will not inherit the kingdom of God. **22** But the fruit of the Spirit is love, joy, peace, patience, kindness, goodness, faithfulness, **23** gentleness, self-control; against such things there is no law. **24** Now those who belong to Christ Jesus have crucified the flesh with its passions and desires. **25** If we live by the Spirit, let us also walk by the Spirit. **26** Let us not become boastful, challenging one another, envying one another.

Travel back and read all of **Galatians 5**. Focus now on this last section, marking **flesh** by shading it any color and **Spirit** with blue wings.

Imagine taking a Sharpie and crossing out **flesh** and **Spirit**. Key words are key words because the text needs them. How different would these verses read if you took them out?

What are your thoughts as to why the flesh and the Spirit are in such opposition?

Complete the following chart based on **Galatians 5:19-23**:

<u>Deeds of the FLESH</u>   vs.   <u>Fruit of the SPIRIT</u>

Provide real life examples for each fruit of the Spirit and how you bring or will bring it into your everyday life to impact the people who surround you. For each fruit, draw a footprint with your action written inside. You must be honest and think about this activity. Studying and reading God's Word is not enough. We must experience transformation and those in our lives must see His Word lived out day to day.

"If you live by the Spirit, walk also by the Spirit." –*Galatians 5:25*

Read **Matthew 15:18-19** below and rewrite it in your own words.

> "But what comes out of the mouth proceeds from the heart, and this defiles a person. For out of the heart come evil thoughts, murder, adultery, sexual immorality, theft, false witness, slander." *–ESV*

How does this compare with The Message translation? Jot down your thoughts.

> "But what comes out of the mouth gets its start in the heart. It's from the heart that we vomit up evil arguments, murders, adulteries, fornications, thefts, lies, and cussing." *–The Message*

Let's get to the heart of the matter. Join **Matthew 15:18-19** with **Galatians 5:19-20**. What is the main thought we are supposed to pull out for our lives?

> "When you follow the desires of your sinful nature, the results are very clear: sexual immorality, impurity, lustful pleasures, idolatry, sorcery, hostility, quarreling, jealousy, outbursts of anger, selfish ambition, dissension, division…" *–NLT*

Don't Stop Yet . . .

Share what you thought was the strongest message Paul was trying to deliver to the church of Galatia.

Share what you thought was the strongest message God was trying to deliver to you this week.

Turning once again to the front of our study, mark all the key words from **Galatians 5**. You marked **God** with a black G, **Jesus Christ** with a red cross, **flesh** by shading it a color, **circumcision** with scissors, and **Spirit** with blue wings.

The heart is what matters – your heart. How was your heart touched this week?

Choose one verse that spoke to your heart and write it below.

Be sure to put it on a 3x5 card for memorization.

A Note From Lisa

We who belong to Christ Jesus have crucified our sinful nature with its passions and desires. Since we live by the Spirit, let us keep in step with the Spirit. May God faithfully unfold His truths to you as you faithfully study Galatians 6. May the Lord make His face shine upon you and be gracious to you.

Sincerely studying God's Word with you,

Going DEEPER STILL in Week 5

WEEK 6: Sow to the Spirit

Read **GALATIANS 1-6**. Then go back and read Galatians 6 again, praying and asking for sight to see His truths.

- As you read Galatians 6, mark **GOD** with a black G.
- As you read Galatians 6 again, mark **JESUS CHRIST** with a red cross.

Continually be on the lookout for **God** and **Jesus Christ**, always marking these two words as you read. The presence of **God** and **Jesus Christ** are pivotal in our faith and in our text.

Lesson 1: Just Do It!

Galatians 6:1-6

1 Brethren, even if anyone is caught in any trespass, you who are spiritual, restore such a one in a spirit of gentleness; each one looking to yourself, so that you too will not be tempted. 2 Bear one another's burdens, and thereby fulfill the law of Christ. 3 For if anyone thinks he is something when he is nothing, he deceives himself. 4 But each one must examine his own work, and then he will have reason for boasting in regard to himself alone, and not in regard to another. 5 For each one will bear his own load. 6 The one who is taught the word is to share all good things with the one who teaches him.

As you walk through each lesson make sure you are sticking to the Word as you think through your answers and the activities.

Mark the two "**if...then**" statements found in this passage of Scripture by underlining them and listing them below.

Today we don't use the greeting of "brethren." When you hear the term "brethren" what do you think of?

Record your definition of **trespass**.

Those who are spiritual are called to do what if they see someone in a trespass?

> "Brothers, if someone is caught in a sin, you who are spiritual should restore him gently. But watch yourself, or you also may be tempted." –*Galatians 6:1, NIV '84*

Whom does "anyone" include? What does "restore" mean to you?

Look below at **Galatians 2:11-14**, and explain the connection, if any, to **Galatians 6:1**.

> "But when Cephas came to Antioch, I opposed him to his face, because he stood condemned. For prior to the coming of certain men from James, he used to eat with the Gentiles; but when they came, he began to withdraw and hold himself aloof, fearing the party of the circumcision. The rest of the Jews joined him in hypocrisy, with the result that even Barnabas was carried away by their hypocrisy. But when I saw that they were not straightforward about the truth of the gospel, I said to Cephas in the presence of all, "If you, being a Jew, live like the Gentiles and not like the Jews, how is it that you compel the Gentiles to live like Jews?"

When have you witnessed someone spiritually restore another with a spirit of gentleness?

Share a right way to restore and a wrong way.

List all Paul's instructions in **Galatians 6:1-6**.

Deeper Still **Take one of Paul's instructions and explain how you might apply it to your life.**

How is the Law of Christ fulfilled in bearing one another's burdens? [Hint: What is the Law of Christ?]

If you are taught the Word, then what is your responsibility?

Use graffiti to fill the space below with all the verbs and nouns from these six verses. Use color and size variation while you have fun! Graffiti is markings, as initials, slogans, or drawings, written, spray-painted, or sketched on a sidewalk, wall of a building or public restroom, or the like.

Read **2 Timothy 3:16-17**. Knowing the truth of 2 Timothy, what do the verbs from your graffiti box signify to you?

"All Scripture is breathed out by God and profitable for teaching, for reproof, for correction, and for training in righteousness, that the man of God may be complete, equipped for every good work." *–ESV*

Lesson 2: _____ << U Name This Lesson!

Galatians 6:7-10

> 7 Do not be deceived, God is not mocked; for whatever a man sows, this he will also reap. 8 For the one who sows to his own flesh will from the flesh reap corruption, but the one who sows to the Spirit will from the Spirit reap eternal life. 9 Let us not lose heart in doing good, for in due time we will reap if we do not grow weary. 10 So then, while we have opportunity, let us do good to all people, and especially to those who are of the household of the faith.

Read **Galatians 6:7-10**. As you read this passage, underline every occurrence of **let us**.

What is Paul instructing?

Illustrate below how you perceive sowing and reaping. How would you define each word and what does it look like?

Now, if we <u>sow to the flesh</u> what will we reap?

And, if we <u>sow to the Spirit</u> what will we reap?

Share an example of either one seen in our world today.

"Those who live only to satisfy their own sinful nature will harvest decay and death from that sinful nature. But those who live to please the Spirit will harvest everlasting life from the Spirit." –*Galatians 6:8, NLT*

Note the BIG contrast in **Galatians 6:8**! Mark the **but** with a square and write out what is being contrasted.

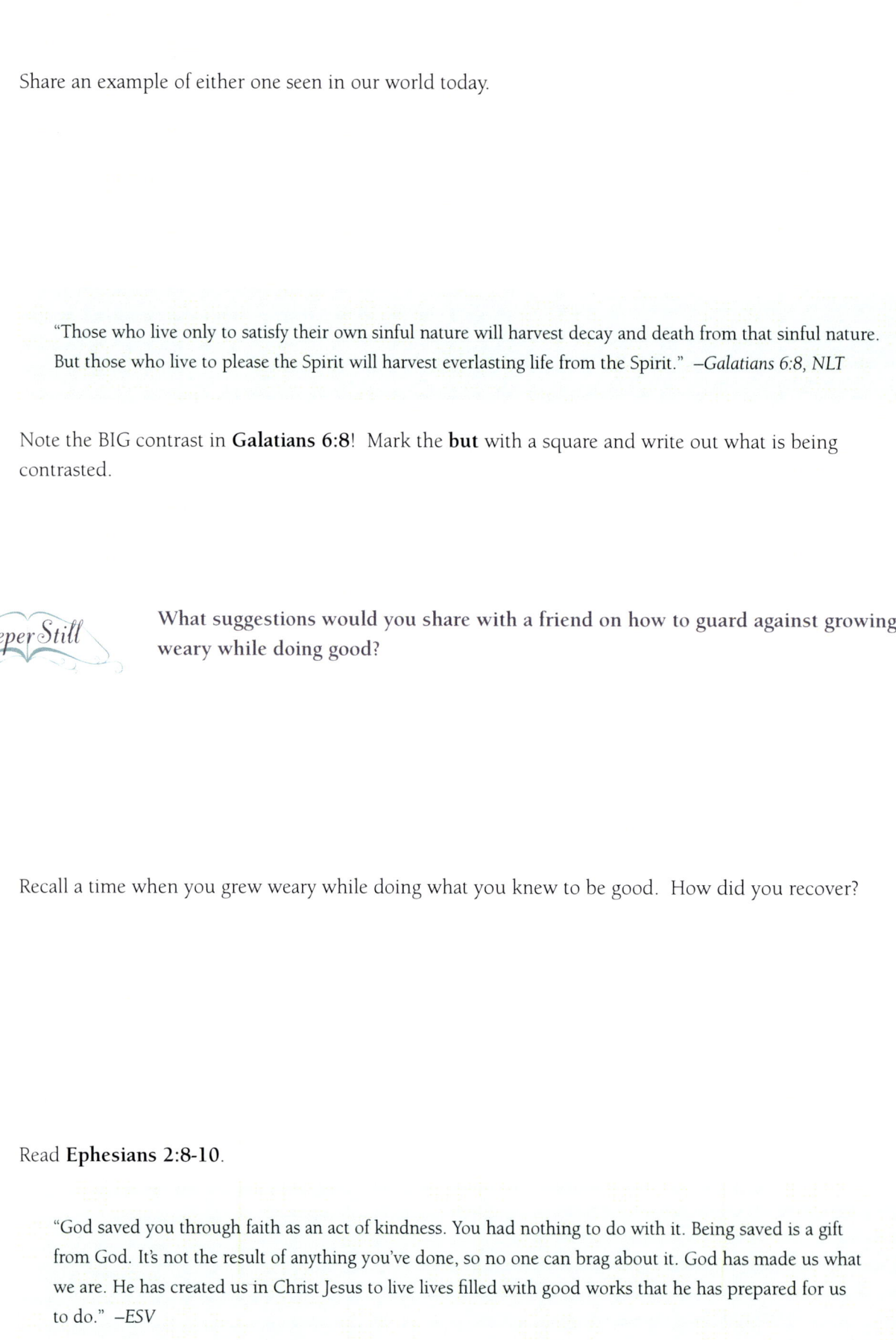

Deeper Still **What suggestions would you share with a friend on how to guard against growing weary while doing good?**

Recall a time when you grew weary while doing what you knew to be good. How did you recover?

Read **Ephesians 2:8-10**.

"God saved you through faith as an act of kindness. You had nothing to do with it. Being saved is a gift from God. It's not the result of anything you've done, so no one can brag about it. God has made us what we are. He has created us in Christ Jesus to live lives filled with good works that he has prepared for us to do." –*ESV*

Rephrase the message Paul is teaching in **Ephesians 2:8-10**.

Join this message with his message in **Galatians 6:9-10** and make a connection with your world.

Create a title for this day's lesson and record it on the line at the beginning of the lesson.

Lesson 3: Walk by This Rule

Galatians 6:11-18

11 See with what large letters I am writing to you with my own hand. 12 Those who desire to make a good showing in the flesh try to compel you to be circumcised, simply so that they will not be persecuted for the cross of Christ. 13 For those who are circumcised do not even keep the Law themselves, but they desire to have you circumcised so that they may boast in your flesh. 14 But may it never be that I would boast, except in the cross of our Lord Jesus Christ, through which the world has been crucified to me, and I to the world. 15 For neither is circumcision anything, nor uncircumcision, but a new creation. 16 And those who will walk by this rule, peace and mercy be upon them, and upon the Israel of God. 17 From now on let no one cause trouble for me, for I bear on my body the brand-marks of Jesus. 18 The grace of our Lord Jesus Christ be with your spirit, brethren. Amen.

Because this is a letter from Paul to the Galatians, I would like to ask you to take a piece of lined notebook paper and pen **Galatians 6**. As you write, think of Paul as he wrote with his own hand with large letters.

To whom do you still write letters? How often do you write to this person? What is the main reason for writing?

Mark **circumcision/circumcised** as you have been. What is Paul's gripe with those who are chasing after circumcision? Travel back to **Galatians 3 and 5** and think about what you have already learned about circumcision. It is important to bring knowledge from one chapter to another.

Boasting, speaking with pride, is a real problem for many when the focus of the boasting is taken off the cross of Christ. Let's practice boasting in the cross of our Lord Jesus Christ. Boast, speak with pride, in the cross of your Lord Jesus Christ below.

Judges 7 tells of a story where God is God and all boasting goes to Him. Write highlights from the story as you read it.

What does Gideon's story have to do with Paul's message in **Galatians 6:14**?

"As for me, may I never boast about anything except the cross of our Lord Jesus Christ. Because of that cross, my interest in this world has been crucified, and the world's interest in me has also died."
–*Galatians 6:14, NLT*

When have you desired to make a good showing in your flesh so that you wouldn't be persecuted for the cross of Christ? Maybe think of a time when you should have stood strong for the cross of Christ but instead you stood strong in your flesh to avoid persecution, teasing, or ridicule. Be honest with yourself.

Through the cross of Jesus Christ, the world has been crucified to Paul and Paul to the world. Explain this to a 13-year-old. Write your explanation in the space provided.

As you reflect on **Galatians 6:15**, what is the only thing that is anything to Paul?

 *Deeper Still* **As we come to the close of Paul's letter, consider what brand-marks of Jesus you bear in your body and record below.**

"Quite frankly, I don't want to be bothered anymore by these disputes. I have far more important things to do—the serious living of this faith. I bear <u>in</u> my body scars from my service to Jesus."
–*Galatians 6:17, The Message*

Don't Stop Yet . . .

Wow! Six weeks of Galatians has proven to be quite a journey.

For the final time, turn to the front of our study and mark all the key words from **Galatians 6**.
You marked **God** with a black G, **Jesus Christ** with a red cross, and **circumcision** with scissors.

What verse will you commit to memory from **Galatians 6**? Articulate why that verse holds such meaning for you that you will commit it to memory.

Take precious time right this moment to read all of **Galatians**. What is a major lesson you learned for your life as you have studied **Galatians**?

After examining **Galatians** in such depth and detail, what would you say is Paul's main reason for communicating with the church in Galatia?

A Note From Lisa

It has been a privilege to travel with you through Paul's letter to the church in Galatia. His letter reveals similarities to the Church today and definite ways to learn and grow. May you be stimulated to grow DEEPER STILL in your walk with your Savior and Lord Jesus Christ. It is my prayer that this will not become just another study you walked through, but will be a walk you will remember, reflect upon, and grow from.

Blessings to you!

Lisa

Going DEEPER STILL in Week 6